MW01250662

Two Indians

Two Indians

Falen Johnson

SCIROCCO DRAMA

Two Indians
first published 2021 by Scirocco Drama
An imprint of J. Gordon Shillingford Publishing Inc.
© 2021 Falen Johnson

Scirocco Drama Editor: Glenda MacFarlane
Cover design by Doowah Design
Author photo by Liz Beddall
Production photos by Cory Dallas Standing, Andy Moro, and Falen Johnson.

Printed and bound in Canada on 100% post-consumer recycled paper.
We acknowledge the financial support of the Manitoba Arts Council and
The Canada Council for the Arts for our publishing program.

Acknowledgements
Thank you to Patrick Bramm for listening,
to Yvette Nolan for always pushing me,
and to the Johnson family for the inspiration.

All rights reserved. No part of this book may be reproduced, for any reason, by
any means, without the permission of the publisher. This play is fully protected
under the copyright laws of Canada and all other countries of the Copyright
Union and is subject to royalty. Changes to the text are expressly forbidden without written consent of the author. Rights to produce, film, record in whole or in
part, in any medium or in any language, by any group, amateur or professional,
are retained by the author.

Production inquiries to:
Ian Arnold at Catalyst TCM Inc
ian@catalysttcm.com

Library and Archives Canada Cataloguing in Publication

Title: Two Indians / Falen Johnson.
Names: Johnson, Falen, 1982- author.
Description: A play.
Identifiers: Canadiana 2021013674X | ISBN 9781927922743 (softcover)
Classification: LCC PS8619.O4613 T96 2021 | DDC C812/.6—dc23

J. Gordon Shillingford Publishing
P.O. Box 86, RPO Corydon Avenue, Winnipeg, MB Canada R3M 3S3

To Naomi.

For teaching me to colour the sky that morning.

Falen Johnson

Falen Johnson is Mohawk and Tuscarora (Bear Clan) from Six Nations Grand River Territory. She is a writer, podcaster, and radio show host. Her plays include *Salt Baby, Two Indians,* and *Ipperwash,* for which she received a Dora Mavor Moore Award nomination for Outstanding New Play. Her writing has been featured in *Brick,* the *Canadian Theatre Review,* and *Granta.* She has also written for *Urban Native Girl* (APTN), *Merchants of the Wild* (APTN) and the 2020 Indspire Awards (CBC). She was named One to Watch in 2020 by *Maclean's* magazine. She co-hosts *The Secret Life of Canada* (CBC Podcasts) with Leah-Simone Bowen and *Unreserved* (CBC Radio One).

Foreword

In January 2016, Tara Beagan asked me if I knew Falen Johnson. We were in Prince George, BC at the time, rehearsing her show *Dreary and Izzy* at Theatre Northwest. My first big theatre gig. I told her no, and she responded, "You need to meet her," adding something about us having a similar sense of humour.

Fast-forward seven months and now it's the opening night of *Two Indians* at the Summerworks Festival in Toronto. Falen and I meet briefly after the show and later we exchange: "Nice to meet you in real life!" "You too, I loved your play and your writing!" messages on Facebook, and then it looks like we didn't talk for two years after that.

I started working at Native Earth Performing Arts doing box of-fice / front of house around this time so I'm sure we ran into each other (I know I worked box office shifts for her show *Ipperwash*) but I find it really funny that the next message Falen sent me was in 2018, when she asked if I was interested in performing in *Two Indians*.

Of course, I said yes.

While we had a short rehearsal period and only two days of performances, this show was good medicine for me. Admittedly, going into it I was having trouble finding my voice and trusting myself as an artist. I felt like Win, just going through the motions, and putting others' needs before my own. But by the end of the process, I remember feeling like a weight had been lifted. I gained back some of the clarity, inner strength, and confidence I had lost for a while. I was reminded of why I love theatre.

Two Indians captures the essence of the community without ever leaving the Toronto alleyway it's set in. Getting to work on such an honest, dialogue-driven show is certainly a highlight for me in my career so far. (It's also harder than it looks to do a two-hander and never leave the stage.)

Two Indians does a really good job of peeling back the layers of personal and familial trauma without feeling rushed, disingenuous, or unnecessary. This is a story that goes exactly where it needs to and doesn't hold back. The journey that Win and Roe take each other on is beautiful to witness. They are two sides of the same coin, and they remind me of my own cousins. Their story is thought-provoking and keeps you on your toes. One second you're laughing and the next you're thinking "Wait… what did they just say?"

I've learned a lot from Falen. In addition to teaching me how to smoke (for theatre!) she's taught me about how to be a better storyteller. Not long after closing our run of the show I asked her to be my mentor for a play I've been working on, and my work is stronger because of her.

Two Indians explores different aspects of life in Canada for Indigenous women. As a young Indigenous woman myself, I'm so glad this story exists. I'm thankful Falen wrote it. And I'm excited for more people to experience it for themselves.

"And we are still here."

Joelle Peters
March 2021

Joelle Peters is an Anishinaabe/Miami actor and playwright from Walpole Island First Nation, Bkejwanong Territory.

Production History

The seeds of *Two Indians* were planted at Wrecking Ball T.O. 14: Idle No More. The short version developed there went on to become this play. Special thanks to the Wrecking Ball team and Native Earth Performing Arts. Thanks also to the Lab Cab Festival for showing the short version of Two Indians. Nia:wen to Aqua, Sarain Carson-Fox, Lena Recollet, Sera-Lys McArthur, and Lia Gomez, who brought the characters to life in that shorter version.

Two Indians was then produced by Salt Baby Collective as a part of the 2016 SummerWorks Performance Festival at the Factory Theatre Studio in Toronto, Ontario with the following team:

Rose (Roe) .... Yolanda Bonnell
Winnie (Win)...................... Darla Contois
Direction .... Jessica Carmichael
Scenography .... Andy Moro
Sound Design
& Original Composition.... Patrick Bramm
Stage Management............. Brittany Ryan
Smoke Dance Instructors .. Courtney Warner
                             & Chris Warner

Another production of *Two Indians* took place for FemFest with Sarasvàti Productions in 2017 with the following team:

Rose (Roe) .... Melanee Deschambeault
Winnie (Win)...................... Erica Wilson
Director............................... Sonya Ballantyne
Designer .... Joseph Abetria
Sound Designer .... Colin Wiens
Stage Management .... Katie Robinson Hoppa

Another showing of *Two Indians* took place at the Gathering Place on Six Nations Reserve as a part of the Onkwehón:we (The Original People's) Festival in 2018 with the following team:

Rose (Roe) .... Samantha Brown

Winnie (Win) .... Joelle Peters

Direction .... Falen Johnson

Scenography Design.......... Andy Moro

Sound Design
& Original Composition.... Patrick Bramm

Stage Management
& Lighting .... Lindy Kinoshameg

In 2019 Gordon Tootoosis Nikaniwin Theatre in Saskatoon produced the show with the following team:

Rose (Roe) .... Candy Renae Fox

Winnie (Win)....................... Andrea Folster

Direction .... Roxanne Dicke

Set Design .... Dannyll Challis

Graffiti Design .... John McDonald

Costume Design .... Denis Rouleau

Production Manager &
Lighting Design.................. Jim Arthur

Sound Design....................... Cory Dallas Standing

Stage Management............. Aaron Shingoose

Dance Choreography......... Tala Tootoosis

Characters

Winnie — "Win"
Rose — "Roe"

Two Mohawk cousins in their mid-to-late 20s.

Production Notes

While this play is set in Toronto, it can really be set anywhere. The cultural references can shift to suit the land the play sits on. One should be mindful of appropriation but if, say, a jingle dance works better than a smoke dance, shift accordingly — just be mindful. The use of the word "Indian" is intentional. I couldn't lie and pretend that we don't talk like that back home. Consider the use of this word, of its power.

Playwright's Note

Two Indians is about ceremony. How we create it with what we have, and how it can be made from memories.

Much of this work comes from my family. Cousins, siblings, aunts and uncles ribbing me around my grandma's dining room table. Reminding me of things that embarrass me. But it also comes from outside, too. From the pain I have seen in the faces of people who lost someone too soon. Or from the rage many Indigenous people express in private and how we express it. How we heal through rage and laughter. These two things can be important medicine.

Roe (Yolanda Bonnell) confronts Win (Darla Contois) about living on the rez.

Win (Darla Contois) listens as Roe (Yolanda Bonnell) defends her choice to leave the rez and move to the city.

Win (Andrea Folster) tells Roe (Candy Renae Fox) that she doesn't like the city smells.

Win (Andrea Folster) attempts to convince Roe (Candy Renae Fox) to come home.

Roe (Candy Renae Fox) tries to convince Win (Andrea Folster) of the merits of city living.

The two cousins, Win (Andrea Folster) and Roe (Candy Renae Fox), watch the moon rise.

Win (Darla Contois) and Roe (Yolanda Bonnell) silhouetted against the moon.

*An alley. Downtown Toronto. Late evening.
June.*

*It's hot. It smells like an alley. We hear
music. It begins, it fades away, and we
hear the sound of streetcars, the occasional
sounds of people having a good time on an
early summer evening. Heading to dinner,
maybe a show. The street sounds run for
the duration of the show. Increasing and
decreasing in various sections.*

*The music and sound swell as we see ROE
(Rose) and WIN (Winnie) walk into the
alley. The alley walls are covered in graffiti
and tags. Milk crates sit in a stack nearby.
There are mysterious alley puddles and
scraps of garbage everywhere.*

*We hear voiceover only; we are not sure if
it is WIN or ROE or both — or someone else
altogether.*

VOICES: Come on, cousin. Little further. You're almost
there. It's just down the road.

As they enter, ROE is speaking.

ROE: I'm trying to convince this guy to buy a pin. On top of all the other shit this guy is buying, leather jackets, sweatshirts, god-awful t-shirts, I'm trying to convince him to buy a goddamn pin. It's so effing ugly too. It's like a, like a pilgrim, like a sexy pilgrim. Her tits are popping out and she's blonde, of course, and she's a sexy pilgrim. She's wearing this like sexy pilgrim outfit. Little black shorts, tall high heel boots, a collar that isn't even connected to a shirt, it's just there to be like sexy. And her hat, her pilgrim hat slightly askew, sexily askew. And she's leaning on this giant guitar. In perfect fuck me pose.

Then all of a sudden it's like I come back into my body, like I land in my skin and I realize how fucking ludicrous this is. I'm an Indian selling pilgrim pins. Sexy pilgrim pins. Sexy rock 'n' roll-themed Thanksgiving pilgrim pins. I know I shouldn't say it, even before I say it, but I just can't stop myself, it's out of my mouth, I look right into this guy's eyes and I say, "Dressed like that no wonder they almost died when they got here."

The guy just looks at me blank. Totally not getting it. And I start giggling and the guy looks at me like what's-so-fucking-funny? And then I start laughing even harder and then I can't stop. And this guy is confused and then offended and then pissed 'cause I just won't stop. Can't stop. And then my manager walks in. I'm on the ground basically pissing myself, tears streaming down my face and I just laugh harder and harder because what else was there to do? I knew I was fucked. Might as well laugh.

ROE laughs, WIN joins in.

WIN:	So what happened?
ROE:	I got a write-up. My manager said it was not the kind of experience that "our" patrons are looking for when they visit one of "our" establishments. Like I'm a stockholder in the company or something. We sell burgers and t-shirts, for christ's sake.

I hate my job.

WIN: Yeah, I'd hate your job too. You work retail in a restaurant. Sounds like a nightmare to me. Why don't you just—

ROE: —why don't I quit?

WIN: Well, yeah.

ROE: Because it pays well, like really, too well. Stupid well for retail. And it is expensive to live here.

WIN: So that is what you moved here for? Retail?

ROE: I moved here for school.

WIN: And now?

ROE: Now I am trying to work in my field.

WIN: Your field?

ROE: Yes.

WIN: You studied art therapy. Seems kinda far away from burger shop retail. And you didn't even finish.

ROE: I almost did. I'm gonna go back. Next semester.

WIN: Sure, if you can get funding again. The band council doesn't like to fund a dropout cousin.

ROE: Yeah yeah yeah. Jesus. I didn't invite you up here to nag me all weekend. And remind me where you are working again?

WIN: It's a good job and at least it's tax-free.

ROE: Slinging smokes to the kids.

WIN: Kids even. Mostly old Indian dudes. Too old to quit.

ROE: Well, you better quit, or you'll end up all old and leathery like those guys. Smelling like a piece of smoked meat.

WIN: Who's nagging now, hey? And what are we even doing here? I didn't come all the way up to your big glorious city to sit in a dirty stink alley.

ROE: No? What'd you come for then?

            A few beats.

WIN: Well, this, I guess.

ROE: Come on. Try and enjoy this. It'll be fun.

            An ambulance drives close by. The siren blares. They pause while they wait for it to pass. WIN looks around.

WIN: This?

ROE: Yeah, dude.

WIN: You wanna tell me why we are here? I see the gross alley. Very impressive. Hooray for pee smell! Can we go now?

ROE: The moon. You will see the moon like never before from right here.

WIN: The moon, cousin?

ROE: Yes, the moon.

WIN: *(Looking around.)* And we gotta do that here? Is this even safe?

ROE: Trust me, they are more afraid of us than we are of them.

WIN: Uh, I don't know about that.

ROE: Just think of them like bears. Make lots of noise and they won't come near you. That's what I do.

WIN: I'm not sure if that's how bears work.

ROE: Come on and rez up.

WIN: What does that even mean?

ROE: You know.

WIN: *(Beat.)* Man, you city Indians.

ROE: What?

WIN: You come up to the city and you act like the moon is this new thing. Like you never seen it before. Like you gotta sit in a dirty alley and see a full moon to feel Indian again. *(Beat.)* You know you can see this kinda thing back home all the time.

            ROE makes a scoffing sound, perhaps a snort.

WIN: What is that supposed to mean?

ROE: Nothing. This is what it's like here. The sky is small here. You gotta plan how you can see things.

WIN: Mmm hmm.

ROE: Oh Jesus, super Indian over here. So what, at home you, what, pack a bundle and head out on the land and wait for the moon to rise over the trees, then empty your menstrual cup in the snow and howl?

WIN: Eww! What is wrong with you?

ROE: When's the last time you even went outside for anything, let alone to see the stars? And going out for a smoke doesn't count.

WIN: I see them all the time.

ROE: On your way home from the smoke shack?

WIN: What's wrong with that? Seeing the stars on my way home from my job? Is that really the worst thing I could do? Look up as I head home or look up when I go for a smoke?

ROE: No, it's not, but don't treat it like you are somehow better than me or like this means less. I didn't know the moon was reserved for the reserved. *(She grins, waits for a response.)*

WIN: Oh, you are clever. Just hilarious.

ROE: Look. I live here now. Three years now. And yeah, it is different, but it's been good for me. It's made me appreciate who I am in a way that home never could. *(She looks up.)* Once you lose the stars you learn to appreciate them.

WIN: Sure.

ROE: I know it's different, but can you just try to enjoy this?

WIN: It stinks. *(She checks her phone.)*

ROE: It stinks everywhere here. You get used to it.

WIN: I don't think I could ever get used to it.

ROE: Sometimes you have to.

WIN: You have to?

She looks to ROE. Silence.

So how long?

ROE: Not long.

Beat.

WIN: So we are here to see the moon.

ROE: Not just any moon. A super moon.

WIN: And what makes it so super?

ROE: It's a really big moon.

WIN: Like a full moon?

ROE: No, it's bigger than that.

WIN: So the moon is closer to the earth? I don't get it.

ROE: Well shit, I don't know, like, the exact science behind it. It's a big moon. It looks big, okay? It's impressive.

WIN: Hold on. *(She pulls out her phone.)*

ROE: Don't do that.

WIN: What? I wanna know. Don't you wanna know what you are out here appreciating?

ROE: No mystery at all.

WIN: *(She Googles on her phone.)* Here. *(She reads from her phone.)* "A supermoon is the coincidence of a full moon or a new moon with the closest approach the Moon makes to the Earth on its elliptical orbit, resulting in the largest apparent size of the lunar disk as seen from Earth. The technical name is the perigee-syzygy of the Earth-Moon-Sun system."

ROE: Well, that's clinical. Could you maybe read that again but this time play some flute music underneath? Drums. An eagle cry.

WIN: *(She continues to look at her phone.)* Okay, so… I need a…

> She looks around the ground for something to draw with. She finds an old can of spray paint and goes to a wall.

So it—

ROE: Whoa!

WIN: What?

ROE: You trying to get arrested?

WIN: Arrested? For this? Seriously? *(Referring to the graffiti and general disrepair of the alley.)* Look around you.

ROE: I know, I know, but shit, if they see you doing that…

WIN: Come on. Rez up.

ROE: *(Beat.)* Fine. I'll watch.

> *Referring to her phone occasionally, WIN begins to draw/paint, as she says the following:*

WIN: Okay, the earth is here. And the moon is here. The moon's orbit is like this. So when it's on this side of the earth it is closer and therefore looks larger. There.

ROE: Mystery solved. You really know how to suck the fun out of things, you know that?

WIN: Sorry.

So we stand here and wait for the moon to rise. Are we even gonna be able to see it from here?

ROE: Oh yeah.

WIN: You do this a lot? Come here?

ROE: Yep. Just about every month. The winter is the best. Snow makes things quieter. Smells less, too.

WIN: And how'd you find this place?

ROE: This old Indian guy who used to stop in the store. He came in once looking for a gift for his niece and we got to chatting. He's from up north. James Bay area. He would come in and we would talk. He had these really sad eyes. Looked like he had a rough time, like he had been crying for a long time. Years maybe. We'd talk. Sometimes even have lunch on my break. He told me about this spot. Told me where to find it. Said he felt like there was something special here.

WIN: So how come he isn't here?

ROE: I don't know. I haven't seen him in a while… He just stopped coming in.

WIN: Maybe he went home.

A few beats.

ROE: Maybe.

WIN: Well, you have some interesting hobbies, cousin.

ROE: Come on, have a seat.

WIN: Where?

ROE: Here. *(She points to the ground.)*

WIN: Ew. No.

ROE: What?

WIN: It's gross. No.

ROE: *(She grumbles.)* Jesus. Fine. Hold on.

> *She looks around, goes to a nearby garbage can, pulls out a newspaper and tosses it on the ground.*

Sit on his face.

WIN: Holy heck. No. I'd rather sit on the ground. I don't know where he's been. *(She points to the politician on the front page.)* And that is a bullshit paper. Have you read some of the comments on their website? That's a paper for racists. Racists read that paper. Racists.

ROE: Oh, just sit down.

> *WIN fusses with the newspaper on the ground for too long, looks around. Finds two milk crates. Fusses with them. Dusts her hands off. Pick up newspapers and sets them on top of the crates. Fusses some more. And finally sits.*

WIN: And now we wait.

ROE: We wait.

                ROE smiles. She sits on a crate.

WIN: We wait.

                We hear the street.

ROE: The other day there was this Indian woman in
                the store. She was the spitting image of Aunty
                Dana. I thought it was her for a second. Little
                and brown, cat shirt, yarn poking out of her
                purse, wearing transition lenses. Just cute
                ,you know. And so I was really helping her.
                Ignoring everyone else in the store. Helping
                her more than I help anyone else. And when
                she gets up to the counter to pay for her stuff
                I ask her if she has a status card and she says,
                "no, not on me," and so I tell her she can use
                mine. And she smiles and I go to get my card
                from my wallet and—

WIN: Doesn't anyone notice when you do stuff like
                that?

ROE: No. God no. Most of the people don't even
                know how deal with tax exemption on the
                computer. There is like, clearly a button.
                Idiots.

WIN: They just don't know. Lots of people don't.

ROE: No. Trust me. Idiots. You haven't met them.

WIN: Well, you gotta teach them.

ROE: I ain't gotta do shit.

WIN: Then they'll never know how to deal with a
                status card. You have to teach them.

ROE: Why is that my job? To teach them?

WIN:	Because no one else will. You know that. Why would they? They'd have to see us then.
ROE:	Are we talking about the same thing here?
WIN:	We are. We have to be the teachers. We do.
ROE:	Here we go.
WIN:	Not here we go.
ROE:	Here we go.
WIN:	Okay, fine. We don't have to. Then who explains? Then no one learns anything and we just disappear.
ROE:	I'm not going anywhere. And do your own work. It's not like I came out of the womb with my history written down in a manual. I had to go looking.
WIN:	I know that.
ROE:	It's not like it doesn't exist. There is stuff out there. It's not even hard to find. You just have to do the work. Read an effing book. Quit asking me to tell you everything in fucking Coles Notes format. I'm tired of trying to find a metaphor that adequately encompasses what went down here. Imagine someone walked into your house and said it was theirs, and then they took your kids away and blah, blah, blah. There isn't a simple way of explaining this. It takes work. It takes undoing. In your own brain. Decolonize yourself.
WIN:	Well, no one is getting on a boat and going home, so I guess we had better find a way to explain their history to them.
ROE:	I just wish they would try.

WIN: I think some of them do.

ROE: I think most of them try their best to forget how they are here. Why there are here. What's been built on our backs.

Like a few weeks ago there was this powwow right beside work. And I just got a pit in my stomach when I saw them setting up. That feeling when you know you are gonna have to deal with it. That "here we go" feeling, that "get ready for it" feeling. And so everybody at work starts bitching and whining about how everyone coming in wants to sit on the patio so they can watch the dancers. One of the guys working the patio actually said to me, "Hey, wagon burner, you should go do a rain dance so we can close the patio and we can all go home early." Right to my face. Right to my face with a powwow happening. He was genuinely confused when I got pissed off. I just can't wait for them to catch up anymore.

WIN: *(She starts to laugh.)* Wagon burner. Jesus. That's funny. Wagon burner. What is this, a John Wayne movie?

ROE: I gotta look at that guy almost every day. And he's the boss's son, so what can I do? Tell on him? Not if I wanna keep my job.

I just feel so angry all the time. Or at least like I'm ready to be angry all the time. Like it is always right there at the door waiting to jump out, almost wanting to jump out.

WIN: I think we all feel like that. Ready to fight. Maybe it's the Mohawk in us. The warrior. Maybe we carry that with us.

ROE: Maybe it's because ten years ago, fuck, five years ago it was all different. No one knew anything and now we have all these white folks lining up to be allies. And they look at me with their eyes all big and full of tears and ask me to absolve their ancestors of something and I am sick of explaining it doesn't work that way. You don't get to cry on me.

WIN: Some people wanna help, is that so bad?

ROE: No. Not really. If we know what that means. I just feel apprehensive. Uneasy with all this sudden "understanding."

WIN: Maybe you are just used to things being so bad it's hard to feel like they are getting better.

ROE: Are they? Getting better? Because we have an acronym for missing and murdered women? I didn't even know it was a thing. Like I knew it was a thing. I knew we were being killed, I knew this, but somehow I didn't, you know? It's like the schools. We grew up fifteen minutes away from one, drove by it more times than I could count, and I didn't know what that building was. I didn't know that our family went there. Because they did so well at hiding it in plain sight from us, they did such a good job of colonizing us that we couldn't see it. I just keep thinking there will be a new headline that explains to me some other atrocity I didn't really know about, but I knew about but I couldn't see. And it will fucking cut right through me. Again.

WIN: Jesus.

        You carry too much. You can't hold all that.

ROE: I'd rather hold it. Try to see it.

       Silence.

       WIN lights a smoke. Exhales.

WIN: How's that working out for you?

       They look at each other. Beat. They laugh.

ROE: I'm just frustrated.

WIN: Oh yeah?

ROE: Shut up. You know what I mean.

WIN: Yeah, I do. I just wonder what frustration gets you.

ROE: It makes me think. It makes me present. It makes me fucking care.

WIN: Why don't you just say what you mean?

ROE: It's different for you. I don't blame you. You live there.

WIN: You don't blame me?

ROE: It makes things different.

WIN: Are you kidding me? You think I don't know that? I know that. I live it.

ROE: I know you know. In some ways. The shitty cellphone signals that drain your battery, you gotta drive half an hour to get groceries, cheap smokes, cheap gas, everybody knows all your business, you'll be able to own a house by the time you're thirty, but you'll never own the land—

WIN: And you think that is the difference? That is what makes here so different from there?

ROE: No, I don't think that is the only thing. I think the apathy is the thing. No one votes or even cares or pays attention to what is happening in the outside world.

WIN: For someone who hasn't been back in years you certainly think you know a lot about us.

ROE: I don't have to go back to know what it's like.

WIN: And now you are all into foreign politics. Voting for their government. Taking part in their systems.

ROE: Yeah, I voted. I didn't want that guy to get in! Fucking dead-eyed soulless zombie. And I wish you would think about voting.

WIN: You vote down home? For band council?

ROE: Do you?

WIN: I don't believe in that system.

ROE: So you are...what, all traditional now? You Longhouse?

WIN: Of course not.

ROE: Then what are you?

WIN: What am I? I am your cousin. I was there when you fell out of that treehouse and broke your arm. I was your human shield on the way to the bus stop everyday between Kindergarten and Grade 12 because you were terrified of the dogs. I taught you to inhale a cigarette and how to forge your mom's signature. I was there when your dad left and you cried and cried. I was there. I was. So why don't you ease up and stop shitting all over a place you don't understand anymore.

ROE:	Whoa.
WIN:	Whoa? *(Beat.)* What, you think you are the only one who can get pissed off? Who is frustrated every goddamn day? I see it, I know it. You're the one who left, so stop acting like that is someone else's fault.

Silence.

ROE:	Sheesh.

Beat.

I missed you.

WIN:	I miss you.

Beat.

ROE:	Thanks for teaching me to smoke. It's been really helpful.
WIN:	You are such a shit.

A silence. WIN lights a smoke.

You ever think of coming back?

ROE:	For what?
WIN:	For anything.
ROE:	I don't know. I feel more myself here than I ever did there.
WIN:	They wish you would. At least to visit.
ROE:	I know. I might.
WIN:	You might?
ROE:	I try.
WIN:	You try? I don't get it.

ROE: Not asking you to.

WIN: It's home.

ROE: Not anymore, it's not. This is home now.

WIN: You have family there.

ROE: Not really.

WIN: Well, screw you, too.

ROE: You know what I mean.

                WIN is silent.

            I can't go back there. I know what they think.
            I know what they see. They can't see me
            without seeing it.

WIN: No one blames you.

ROE: Yeah. I find that hard to believe.

WIN: You blame you.

ROE: They can't say they blame me. They probably
            aren't trying to. Maybe they don't even really
            want to. I know that. But it's there. I see it. The
            way they look at me. There is this sympathy,
            this sadness. I'm not who I used to be. I'm a
            ghost, cousin.

WIN: Just because you were in the car doesn't mean
            you died too.

ROE: You're right. And here, in the city, I can be
            alive; there I am a reminder. I can't live being
            a tombstone.

WIN: Well. I guess this was for nothing then.

ROE: This?

                WIN is silent.

ROE: This visit? Your big trip to the city as family ambassador to try and make me go back?

Silence.

What, you didn't think I knew? You are so fucking obvious. .Come on. We haven't spoken... since...hmm...let me think. When was that? When was that? When could that have—

WIN: Jesus. Could you not? I'm not the enemy here. What is your problem?

ROE: Because I went and because I am the one who left, so no one has to try. No one has to care. I left, so it's my fault, so no one has to call or visit. So if I don't go home, if I don't call, then I am the dick. I am the inconsiderate asshole who gave up, who doesn't care, but it's a two-way street. It takes three years for the family ambassador to grace me with an appearance.

WIN: Is this not trying? Sorry, but you are just one person. We can't all come running, we have lives too, no matter how fucking small they may look to you. Why don't you just go to another rally to feel like you are a part of something?

ROE: It'd be more than you've ever done. At least I try.

WIN: 'Cause you have a medicine wheel button on your backpack? You hold hands with hippies who say they understand us? I see your Facebook pics. Way to go to a rally. Shit, you are trying so hard. Here, why don't you go and make a picket sign with a clever slogan that changes the world.

WIN tosses the spray paint at ROE.

ROE: When did you get so mean?

WIN: When did you turn so soft?

ROE: Soft? This is soft? You have no idea what I live every day.

WIN: You're right, I have no idea. How could I? You can't even fucking call home to even tell us if you are still alive!

ROE: This is how you get me to go home? By being an asshole? Hey, did you think that maybe it wasn't the accident?

WIN: Did I ever think that what wasn't the accident?

ROE: Why I don't come home.

WIN: Oh really, then why? Please enlighten me.

ROE: Because here I get to be me in a bigger way than I could ever there, and how could I not like that? And it is such a goddamn mess down there.

WIN: And it isn't here? Look at this place. Look how you live. You live in a basement with no windows. You can barely afford to eat.

ROE: Well, at least I can drink the water.

WIN: Oh, fuck off, we haven't had to boil in years.

ROE: *(Laughs.)* Can you hear yourself?

WIN: Nah. I don't buy it.

ROE: What?

WIN: "You are more yourself." No. You're afraid. And you know what? I get it.

ROE:	No. No, you don't. You don't get it. You can't. You could never. They are dead and I watched it happen and I am supposed to keep living. You weren't there.
WIN:	And there, there it is!
ROE:	There what is?
WIN:	You are right, I wasn't there. You'd prefer it if I was. You'd prefer if it was me instead of Christine or Seth or Ray Anne in that car.
ROE:	No! Don't say shit like that. I didn't— I don't want that.
WIN:	You guys didn't even want me to come. You never did. I hate bush parties and you all knew that. I was terrible at them. Sat alone somewhere doing my best to not get hit on by some creep that is probably related to us, while you guys partied. That night, when you told me there wasn't room in the car, I knew there was. I knew. And I knew that you guys had finally gotten sick of dragging me around. But I didn't care. I got so sick of pretending to have fun with you guys.
ROE:	I... I...didn't want you to come. I didn't. None of us did. You were terrible at those things, but I didn't want to hurt your feelings by not inviting you. I'm glad you weren't there. I'm glad you wanted to stay home. I am glad we lied to you. And I am glad you are here now.
WIN:	I am here and so are you. They died and I learned to live without them, but I didn't think I was gonna have to live without you too. We just want you to visit. It would mean a lot to Grandma.

ROE: Three of her other grandkids are gone because of me. I can't forget that. And neither can she.

WIN: Three. Not four. Don't take another one away from her. Don't do that to her. She raised you. You owe her.

ROE: Hey cousin, how come Indians always die in cars? Is it like the new diabetes or something?

WIN: That's not funny.

ROE: It kind of is.

        Those roads. I know them like the back of my hand. The curves, the bumps, the potholes that come up after the rain. I know them.

        You know, I see them sometimes.

WIN: The roads?

ROE: The cousins.

WIN: You do? Where?

ROE: Wherever it's busy. The street during rush hour downtown, the subway, the mall when I'm on my lunch. I see flashes of their faces for a split second and then they are gone. Lost in a crowd. I wish I could forget that they are dead long enough to really think it's them. To really give over, you know? I'd like to forget for a few seconds.

WIN: I saw them once. All three of them in a dream. Right after it happened.

                Silence.

ROE: You never told me that.

WIN: I wasn't sure you'd wanna hear it.

ROE: Of course I wanna. I want to now.

WIN: In my dream I woke up on the couch in
            Grandma's house. That old grey one. I sat
            up and looked around for Grandma and
            I couldn't see her anywhere but I could
            hear the clock ticking. That damn loud
            clock she has. Tick tick tick. And I could
            smell something baking. Weird to smell in
            dreams but I could. It was cookies or bread
            or something, something in the oven. I
            walked into the kitchen and they were there,
            the cousins. They stood at the height chart
            against the wall measuring each other to see
            who had grown the tallest since they last
            checked. I don't know why they would. We
            all stopped growing a long time ago, but
            they stood there, Seth kept going up on his
            toes and Christine kept yelling at him to quit
            cheating, Ray Anne just kept giggling kinda
            nervous the way she always did. And they
            noticed me. All of them at the same time. And
            for a second, they stood looking at me and
            then like a silent agreement between them
            they grabbed me and pushed me against
            the wall. They were laughing and they were
            trying to hold me against the wall to measure
            me. They kept pushing me and it got really
            rough and I tried to get them to let me go but
            they wouldn't. I got scared and I didn't know
            what to do so I yelled, "You are dead! Leave
            me alone! You guys are dead." And they
            stopped and backed away. Then they started
            laughing even harder than before. And it got
            really deep-sounding, not like their voices
            at all. I covered my ears and closed my eyes
            and went to scream but I couldn't. I opened
            my eyes and they were gone. I was still in the
            kitchen and I could still smell the cookies or
            whatever and hear the clock, but they were

gone. I turned and looked at the height chart and their lines were gone. I could see you and me but they weren't there anymore. I walked back into the living room and you were there with Grandma. You guys were picking lint off of the carpet in the front room, you both looked at me and smiled and I woke up.

ROE: *(Beat.)* Wow. What do you think that means?

WIN: I don't know. I don't think it really matters. She still has it, you know.

ROE: Has what?

WIN: That damn loud clock.

ROE: I'm not surprised.

WIN: And she still has your grad picture hanging right beside it.

ROE: *(Genuine surprise.)* Yeah?

WIN: I graduated with honours and yet you still get top billing somehow.

ROE: Sucker. *(Beat.)* Does she still pick lint off the carpet like that? On her hands and knees?

WIN: ·   Her knees are too bad now. Must bug her. My dad got her a new vacuum, but she says it makes her hearing aid ring.

> *An ambulance or fire truck siren; they wait. ROE picks up spray paint and measures her height. She motions for WIN to come and do the same. She does.*

ROE: Well, I may have top billing beside the clock, but you will always be taller.

WIN: At least I have that.

ROE beings to draw a tree on the alley wall.
It encompasses the height lines.

WIN: You know what my earliest memory is of
Christine? Well, not of her, but with her. I
must have been three or four. Really little.
She stayed over one night and we woke up
early in the morning, before anyone else was
up and we watched the sun come up. It was
fall time so the trees were bare. But the sky
was orange and pink and blue and beautiful.
We got my crayons and she showed me how
to blend the colours into each other, from
yellow to orange to pink to blue. She showed
me how to draw tree branches thin and black
against the bright sky. She told me I was good
and I believed her. I felt proud of myself.
She was so good at drawing I used to be so
jealous. I used to want to be like her so badly.

She stops drawing, staring at the tree. ROE
is lost in memory.

Remember that time her and Seth got in that
fight?

ROE: Which one?

WIN: The baseball one! When Seth and Christine
argued over if the ball was foul or fair. And
Christine kept yelling, "FOUL" and Seth kept
screaming, "FAIR" right in her face. Until he
got so mad he punched the side of Grandma's
house and broke his hand.

ROE: Oh my god, I totally forgot about that.

WIN: Really?! God, it's my favourite. That guy was
always hurting himself. That time he put his
fingers in the blender.

ROE: Remember that time when Ray Anne was just little and she got stuck in the toilet? No one even helped her, everyone just went looking for their cameras.

WIN: Oh god. I love those pictures.

They both laugh.

ROE: I miss them so much.

WIN: Every day.

ROE: Never seen a sky like that morning. Never felt proud of myself like that again. Not like that morning.

I don't want to die in a car.

WIN: You won't.

ROE: You can't promise that.

WIN: Well, you can't walk through life thinking you're gonna die every time you get in a car.

ROE: *(She motions to her surroundings.)* Public transit, cousin.

WIN: And this is all you want for the rest of your life?

ROE: For now, yes.

WIN: You have to come home. At least for a visit. Grandma isn't gonna be around forever and you will hate yourself if you don't come. And I will hate you for breaking her heart. I'm here now, but if you don't promise me you will come for a visit, I don't know…

ROE: Threats now?

WIN: You know what, here.

WIN pulls out her phone.

ROE: What? What are you doing?

WIN beings to scroll through her contacts.

What are you doing?!

WIN: You can tell her. I'm not.

ROE: Put it away.

WIN: *(She dials.)* Here. You can tell your grandma that—

ROE: Put it away!

ROE goes to grab the phone. They struggle.

Stop!

ROE grabs the phone and it is thrown to the ground in the struggle. They stop. Beat.

WIN: WHAT THE FUCK?! You asshole! Do you know how much those things cost?! You better hope it isn't broken.

She goes to her phone and picks it up.

What the hell is your problem?!

ROE: You made me! It was an accident!

WIN: You know, maybe you should just stay here, sit in your big fucking city looking down on all of us back home. We don't need your shit anyway. Have a great life being "more yourself."

WIN begins to leave.

You've always been kind of an asshole; you being here just makes it worse.

ROE: You don't know! You don't know what this is like.

WIN: *(She stops.)* Yeah, I don't know. I can't know. You survived and that means something. But I can't make you see it.

ROE: You think you know everything, but you don't.

WIN: I don't think I know everything. I think I know you. And I think I know that you should come home for visit. And that is all I know. That's it!

ROE: I told them it was me.

WIN: You told who it was you?

ROE: I told them it was me. I told them I was driving.

WIN: Yeah? And?

ROE: The accident. I wasn't driving. It wasn't me. It was Christine. I told them it was me.

WIN: What? Why?

ROE: When I woke up in the hospital, even before I opened my eyes, I heard them crying in the hallway. The whole family. I knew then that they were gone. All three of them. I knew. I remembered the night and what had happened. I remembered seeing the tree come to us. I know that doesn't make sense, for the tree to come to us, but I saw it. It grabbed us. Reached for us. And then we all flew for a second, suspended. Ray Anne's hair brushed my face and I remember smelling her shampoo, Christine was trying to cover her face, and Seth looked so scared. So scared. I hated seeing that. I could smell smoke and gas and glass was everywhere and remember thinking about you. And I thought, at least Win isn't here.

WIN: But everyone said you were driving. That's what they said.

ROE: She was drunk. Christine was drunk. And I let her drive.

I was supposed to drive but she wouldn't let up. She kept pushing and pushing and we were just going down the road. Just a few houses. Just down the road. Just down the road, cousin. So I let her. And Seth called shotgun so I sat in the back behind Christine and Ray Anne was behind Seth.

When I woke up in the hospital and heard crying, that wailing crying. Aunty Dana was screaming Christine's name over and over, I heard her ask who was driving, who was driving. I wanted to do something to make it stop. So when they asked me what happened I said it was me. I said I was driving. None of us were wearing belts, we all flew everywhere. I figured they must not have been able to tell. No one said anything. No one challenged me. Even if they didn't believe me none of it mattered because no one said anything.

That fall I came up here to go to school and I just stayed.

WIN: Why would you do that? Why would you lie about something like that?

ROE: Christine was good. She had so much good in her and I didn't want her life, her memory to be reduced to a drunk Indian who crashed and killed herself and her cousins.

WIN: And you want that for you?

ROE: No, I didn't, but I am so far in, I don't exactly know how to turn back. I'm not sure I want to at this point. And I let her drive; I did that.

WIN: Now you are up here thinking what? That you are doing some amazing noble thing for Christine? For the family?

ROE: After all this time does it make sense to tell? After everyone has finally stopped crying?

WIN: You could have told me. You could have told me something. Anything. Instead you left, leaving me to hold everything and everyone together. Do you know how hard that was? How hard it still is?

        And here you are protecting the dead cousin while I struggle every goddamn day. You think that this is what I wanted? To turn down going to school, to put my life on hold 'cause I was too afraid of what would happen if I left? And you. You sit up here a dropout. Complaining about your life, about what you chose.

ROE: I didn't think you even wanted to leave.

WIN: I never had a choice! *(Beat.)* I didn't come here to drag you home. I came here to tell you I can't do this anymore. Not without help. Not without you. I can't keep paying for the decisions you made.

        ROE is silent.

        I am not asking you to come have some big family reunion. I am asking you to just come. You don't even have to see anyone yet. Just take this first step.

ROE: You're right. I am afraid.

WIN: So am I. But I need you now. I think we need
                each other.

ROE: Okay.

WIN: Okay.

ROE: I'll come.

WIN: Yeah?

ROE: Yeah.

                They embrace.

                Hey, you got a smoke?

WIN: Yeah. Thought you quit, though.

ROE: I did.

                *WIN pulls out her pack and gives ROE a
                cigarette. ROE rips it in half and empties
                the tobacco out. She motions to WIN to
                come. She gives her half the tobacco and
                walks near the tree/height chart drawing
                and looks at her cousin and places it down.
                WIN does the same.*

                It ain't ceremonial, but it'll have to do.

WIN: It does.

                *They take a moment looking at the tree.
                The street sounds in the background grow.
                It is a streetcar or the sounds of someone
                shuffling. It mimics the sounds of a rattle or
                a drum with a smoke dance rhythm. WIN
                hears it. Slowly she begins to move.*

                Come on. *(She laughs.)*

ROE listens for a moment, then understands what it is.

ROE: No fucking way.

WIN: Come on.

ROE: No.

WIN: I was always better anyways. Always won.

ROE: No. You didn't. Christine always won. She was championship.

WIN: Never let us forget it.

ROE: Forced us to learn so she could practise beating us.

WIN: Come on.

ROE: No way. Not here.

WIN: You forget?

ROE: No. Not a chance.

WIN: You're just afraid 'cause I always beat you.

ROE: No. You didn't.

WIN: Prove it.

ROE: You prove it.

WIN: That doesn't make any sense. Come on.

ROE: There isn't any music.

WIN: *(In her Indian voice.)* Come on, cousin. Feel the rhythm of your heart. *(She pounds her chest stoically.)*

ROE: Oh my god, stop. Why don't you go paint with all the colours of the wind.

WIN:	Okay here, here, here.

WIN pulls out her phone, scrolls and plays a song. It has the feel of a smoke dance song but isn't. It works. WIN begins to dance, slow but building.

Come on. Come on, cousin. You owe me after trying to break my phone.

ROE: Oh Jesus, you are for real. All right. Let's go.

She begins to dance. She finds her rhythm after some time and they both begin to speed up, challenging each other.

WIN: Oh man, you are rusty!

ROE: Don't try and distract me!

WIN: Is it that easy?

ROE: Stop!

WIN: Slow. Slow. Slow. And I'm the smoker!

ROE dances harder. Faster. They sync up and fall apart. They laugh and dance. Without them noticing, the moon begins to rise over them. As the light hits their faces they stop and look out. The music changes, either slows or fades. Shadows grow behind them and we can't tell which one is Roe's and which is Win's. More shadows appear and grow and dance behind the cousins. The tree where the height lines are develops three new lines of varying heights. They are for Christine, Seth and Ray Anne.

Holy shit.

ROE: I mean, I don't wanna say I told you so, but…

WIN: Shut up!

WIN slaps ROE's arm.

ROE: Ow!

WIN: Rez up.

WIN wraps her arm around ROE. ROE responds. They stand watching the moonrise.

WIN: At least there's still this.

ROE: And we are still here.

WIN: We are.

END